"Outstanding! An unbelievably accurate depiction of the process of discipleship! Alvin has addressed the thoughts of so many New Christian Converts!"
David M. –Maryland


"This concept is amazing! Alvin is exactly right in his Slow-cooking process in discipleship!"
Linda G. –Maryland


"I LOVE, LOVE, LOVE this book! The Crockpot Christian is engaging, relevant and easy to understand!
Melissa R. –North Carolina

Alvin T. Harmon Jr.

# The Crockpot Christian: *A Simple Guide to Christian Discipleship*

Alvin T. Harmon Jr.

The Crockpot Christian: A Simple Guide to Christian Discipleship
Published by Soul House Ministries Inc.,
517 Ellison Court Frederick, Maryland 21703

Library of Congress Control Number: 2012918459

ISBN-10: 0615705391

ISBN-13: 978-0-615-70539-2

Printed in The United States of America

2012 First Edition

# DEDICATION

*I have dedicated this book to my wife and friend Tineka. Who has consistently been strength for me. She helped me to realize that genuine Christianity could never be an overnight process.*

Alvin T. Harmon Jr.

# The Crockpot Christian: *A Simple Guide to Christian Discipleship*

Alvin T. Harmon Jr.

# CONTENTS

# ACKNOWLEDGMENTS

With special thanks:

- ♥ To my Lord and Savior Jesus Christ, who has saved my life by saving my soul. Through the Holy Scriptures; He is the foundation of discipline.

- ♥ To my wife Tineka, who has been the structure and balance in my life. I could never show you the true value of my appreciation.

- ♥ To my children Damel, Davell, Joshua, Junia and Daniel, thank you for helping me to gain focus in life. You have been true inspiration in all I do.

# INTRODUCTION

In the age of 4G, microwaves and 24 hour news, it is sometimes hard to perceive the concept of good 'ole fashion patience. It is 2012 and my mother still uses dial-up and the conventional oven.

I would ask her why but I already know her answer; because she can wait. As a born again Christian I understood all too well the pressures associated with the quick Christian transformation.

I came from a doctrine that taught the instantaneous Christian. It enforced the fact that once you accepted Jesus Christ as savior, you must immediately stop all sin. However, it did not continue to explain how or the possible amount of difficulty that it may prove to present. In my humble opinion, it may have led me and many alike to perceive a Christian walk with a false sense of reality.

At the point when you understood how you were dealing with any flaw or condition associated with sin; you would try to do all you could to prevent the seemingly shameful looks of condemnation that you were sure would follow.

Don't misunderstand me, I believe that we must stop all forms of sin but I also believe that to expect it done in a single moment is to say at the least "challenging."

**2 Peter 3:8** (CEV)
Dear friends, don't forget that for the Lord one day is the same as a thousand years, and a thousand years is the same as one day.

Therefore, that which seems to us as a lifetime of struggling *to get it right* is only a few days to God.

Use patience and persistence, choose value and vigilance and allow God to do the rest!

Throughout the 15 years beyond my accepting Christ as savior and Lord, I realized that there was so much that I needed to "lie down" or "set aside."

If Christian means "Christ-like," then I sure didn't fit the mold after my announcement of salvation.

I wanted to become "like" Jesus but I definitely wasn't there yet. I was always taught that Jesus defeated sin in the flesh to *show us* that we should and "could" do the same.

Even his disciples who were with him, had to receive continual correction as they were "walking" with Jesus or along the way.

**Mark 10:13-16** (CEV)

[13] Some people brought their children to Jesus so that he could bless them by placing his hands on them. But his disciples told the people to stop bothering him.

[14] When Jesus saw this, he became angry and said, "Let the children come to me! Don't try to stop them.

People who are like these little children belong to the kingdom of God. [15] I promise you that you cannot get into God's kingdom, unless you accept it the way a child does." [16] Then Jesus took the children in his arms and blessed them by placing his hands on them.

Jesus Himself was patient for three years with twelve men who accepted Him and watched Him on a daily basis. How can we honestly expect those of us who have not seen to become Christ-like overnight?

I've just accepted Jesus as Savior. Now what? Well, it is sad to say that many new converts, will begin a life-long walk without genuine direction.

I offer to you a solution which suggests that there is a divide from accepting Christ as Lord and Savior and becoming Christ-like or Christian. That divide is called Discipleship.

Discipleship is the key. It is the period of time that it takes to form the discipline necessary to become Christ-like.

Now, that time period cannot and will not be the same for every born-again believer. However, if a believer is genuine about their will to become Christ-like then you should see a person who is ever evolving. A person whose attributes and characteristics begin and continue to resemble those of Jesus, The Christ.

## The Solution

I will share with you a "slow-cooking" concept that will take you step-by-step into functional and practical Christianity.

This book does not focus on Spirituality alone because I believe that each individual's personal relationship with God is exactly that.

However, I will relate some spiritual notations and examples where they may prove to magnify an idea or help define an expression.

Disclaimer: Although I have made earlier references to "cooking" a Christian; I in no means have engaged in nor encourage the real acts of placing or attempting to place any persons, Christian or other, into a pot of any type for cooking!

# CHAPTER 1

## PLAN YOUR MEAL

| Sun | Mon | Tue | We | Thu | Fri | Sat |
|-----|-----|-----|-----|-----|-----|-----|
|     |     |     |     |     |     | 1   |
| 2   | 3   | 4   | 5   | 6   | 7   | 8   |
| 9   | 10  | 11  | 12  | 13  | 14  | 15  |
| 16  | 17  | 18  | 19  | 20  | 21  | 22  |
| 23  | 24  | 25  | 26  | 27  | 28  | 29  |
| 30  | 31  |     |     |     |     |     |

As young disciples, we were always taught that God was "The Master Planner." This was a theory which suggested that God expected us to have no ideas or concepts of our own.

This thought process lead us to perceive that we were to sit and wait for Him to manifest every good thing in our lives.

God was to choose our houses, our vehicles and even our spouses. Some even made mention that God needed to choose what we were going to wear for the day.

I'm not talking about merely being open to His influence but literally expecting God to make these practical decisions for us.

The scripture that was used to solidify this instruction came out of the **Proverbs 3:6**. *In all thy ways acknowledge him, and he shall direct thy paths.* Eh hem! I'll just say reading the entire third chapter in context, permits us to see that God was ***not*** focused on houses and daily apparel.

There was absolutely no need for planning because God had it all under control. The term "Master Planner" itself suggest that there are sub-planners or under planners of some form.

There may be either an apprentice planner or a journeyman planner. There is the master chef who trumps the sous chef or the prep cook.

The point is that these all work and plan as part of the Masters design. Now, with that being said, we do not always plan properly.

When The Master sees that something did not go according to His plan, He comes back to us and makes corrections as He did with Adam and Eve.

In the second and third Chapters of Genesis we understand that God's plan was for Adam and Eve to mind the Garden of Eden and to not eat the fruit from **ONE** particular tree.

He never told Adam how to mind the garden. As a matter of fact, if you read the second chapter closely you will see that He told Adam to eat from *any* other tree except from the one in the middle of the garden.

God made animals for Adam to name and made him a wife to help. God had left all of the planning of "all things Garden" to Adam. It was only when Adam's plan did not line up with the Master Plan that God had to come and make some corrections.

God took them out of the garden and made Adam go work (farm) the very ground from which he's made. God wants us to plan but as a part of His Master Plan.

Jesus said in **Luke 14:28-30**(CEV) [28] Suppose one of you wants to build a tower. What is the first thing you will do? Won't you sit down and figure out how much it will cost and if you have enough money to pay for it? [29] Otherwise, you will start building the tower, but not be able to finish. Then everyone who sees what is happening will laugh at you. [30] They will say, "You started building, but could not finish the job."

Today, we see a lot of Christians in the public arena who started building but could not finish the job. Primarily, because they didn't sit down to figure it all out.

They never figured out if they had enough to pay for the life they were building. I'm not speaking of money but of enough character and discipline. They didn't plan their meal.

"My meal" is interpreted as; my result or the type of person I want to become and the type of life I want to live. I am of the opinion, that God allows us to make free will decisions concerning our lives and livelihood.

I can choose to become a lawyer, mechanic or an airline pilot. He just requires us to make Him our focal point in all we do.

Understanding, that we do not allow our desires to lead us away from our personal service and dedication to God.

Example: After all is complete, my "meal plan" will show me as a man of (1) Integrity, (2) Honesty, (3) Loyalty, (4) Humility, (5) an Entrepreneur, (6) a man of unwavering Faith, (7) Compassionate and (8) an obedient servant of God.

I have listed eight personal characteristics that I, through biblical influence, wanted prevalent in my life. Some are spiritual, some social and practical. Just *stay honest* in planning your own.

These characteristics translate into my meal courses. I have just planned an eight course meal. Each course will be made differently. There will be variances in prep times, as well as cook times.

Now, that you know what your "meal" will be we will move on to the next step.

CHAPTER 2

## CLEAR THE OLD AND SET THE NEW!

After planning a meal, most cooks would first run out and shop for all the ingredients used in each course. As children of faith our next step is to *Clear And Set The Table.*

Why? Well, the answer is very simple. It is the act of preparation that excites God!

**Hebrews 11:6** (CEV) But without faith no one can please God. We must believe that God is real and that he rewards everyone who searches for him.

By doing this, we show God and ourselves that there ***will*** be a meal prepared and thereby activating our faith.

We want to clear the old table and set the new! That means we are clearing away or removing the old and unwanted habits and characteristics or the things about our current state which prevent us from getting to our result.

**Hebrews 12:1** Such a large crowd of witnesses is all around us! So we must get rid of everything that slows us down, especially the sin that just won't let go. And we must be determined to run the race that is ahead of us.

*To begin with, choose **_one_** unwanted habit that you wish to eliminate or change. Then, choose a desired habit you want to adopt as part of your behavior. If it is a habit to eliminate, you may wish to go "cold turkey" or have a gradual tapering off.

Caution: If it is a drug or chemical habit you are planning on eliminating, be sure to obtain an expert's opinion as to whether you need to taper off usage as opposed to quitting cold turkey.

Example:

If one of my "courses" was to achieve honesty and I am not always truthful or I have a deceitful nature, then I want to clear deceitfulness and lying from my table.

I will no longer tell lies or be deceitful. The key to any of this working to your best benefit is to be complete honesty about your faults and flaws.

Sometimes, it takes a bit of digging and uprooting or even considering previously disregarded comments from friends and family members.

All of which may prove to inflict injury on one's pride. So, be prepared to bite down hard. Without this level of personal honesty, you will be wasting your time.

*Now that you have decided which unwanted habit to eliminate or new habit to adopt, decide on the date you will begin your

behavior change. Give this date a good deal of thought and then write it down. For example; "On October 20th, 2012 I will become a non-smoker."

*In order to ensure behavior change, experts agree that it takes a minimum of 21-28 days to change a behavior. Again, look at the date you are planning on changing your habit. Count ahead 21-28 days and mark that date down. Now, commit to follow your plan for 21-28 days.

**Helpful Suggestions**

*Your target date has arrived. It is the first day of your 21-28 day cycle. Here are some helpful suggestions for habit change:

1.  *Write down your goal. There is magic in the written word when it applies to you. Experts recommend

stating your goal in positive terms, such as "I want to be lean and physically fit," instead of "I've got to get this flabby body out there huffing and puffing." So, begin

with writing down, as a positive goal, the habit you will change.

**Habakkuk 2:2** (AMP)

And the Lord answered me and said, Write the vision and engrave it so plainly upon tablets that everyone who passes may [be able to] read [it easily and quickly] as he hastens by.

**Also, as crazy as it may seem, visualize and vocalize your results!**

**Romans 4:16-18** (AMP)

[16]Therefore, [inheriting] the promise is the outcome of faith and depends [entirely] on faith, in order that it might be given as an act of grace (unmerited favor), to make it stable and valid and guaranteed to all his descendants--not only to the devotees and adherents of the Law, but also to those who share the faith of Abraham, who is [thus] the father of us all.

[17]As it is written, I have made you the father of many nations. [He was appointed our father] in the sight of God in

whom he believed, who gives life to the dead and speaks of the nonexistent things that [He has foretold and promised] as if they [already] existed.

[18][For Abraham, human reason for] hope being gone, hoped in faith that he should become the father of many nations, as he had been promised, So [numberless] shall your descendants be.

2 &ast;List your reasons for changing or eliminating your habit. Writing it down will force you to think out in specific terms what this habit represents in your life and the meaning you believe your life will hold for you upon changing the habit. This will also help with your commitment toward taking positive action.

We cannot just leave it at clearing away the deceit and lies we must also introduce the replacement behavior.

3 Find substitute behaviors. For example, where ever you feel the need to tell a lie, no matter what it may cost you personally, just tell the truth! I know. I know. That's seems scary right? But after truth-telling becomes a rock solid and genuine life behavior for you, it will bring so much gratification. Not just to you, but to God and others in your life.

4   *Talk to yourself. Tell yourself you're making progress. Remind yourself that you are moving closer to your goal... Talk to yourself throughout the day about how you are going to avoid triggers that can get you off track and make healthy substitutes.

5   *Recruit helpers for support. Explain to them why you are making this change. Ask for their support. Their support may be needed encouragement.

6   *Be prepared for adverse people or situations who may attempt to sabotage your change. Be assertive and tell them what they are doing.

## Sustaining Motivation

*The following are some suggestions to follow each day in order to sustain motivation and determination:

1.   *Review your list of reasons for quitting or changing.

2.   *Create mental pictures of yourself as having already succeeded with your habit change.

3.  *Make affirmations, positive self-statements about your habit change. For example, "I am filled with so much health and vitality now that I exercise four times a week."

4.  *Reward yourself. Make up a list of self-rewards. Reward yourself verbally.

5.  *Remember to take one day at a time. If you do backslide, don't label yourself as having failed. Get out your list or reasons for quitting or changing and begin again.

*Fatigue, boredom, depression, stress can all make it difficult to stick with your program. But having a relapse isn't as important as how you deal with the relapse.

If you are so devastated by failure that you call your good intentions into question, it will make habit change harder for you.

Also, if you allow for an occasional relapse and treat it as nothing more than a slight misstep that teaches you something, then you're on the right track.

*Follow these suggestions, adopt the more helpful attitude of evaluating your progress and accepting relapses, and you will find yourself reaching many of your goals. You will have achieved true behavior change.

**\*© 2003 Office of Employee Assistance/Florida International University.**

Now let's chart our "courses" (so to speak), by individualizing them. Let's start small and work our way to more difficult courses.

Then later, get some relief from our more complicated unwanted habits (because we don't want to overwhelm ourselves) by working on some extra smaller "courses" as a finale.

The following course statements ***are all*** suggestions. They are just to be used as a template for your individual situations.

# WRITE THE VISION

_____

_____

_____

_____

_____

_____

_____

_____

_____

_____

_____

_____

_____

_____

_____

_____

_____

_____

CHAPTER 3

## APPETIZERS

### (JUST TO GET YOU STARTED)

Freedom from Gossip

**Prep time:** Dedicate at least forty-five minutes to find scripture(s) to support removing your old behavior and introducing the new. Also, if necessary find a support person to cheer you on!

Cook time: 21-28 Days

**Ingredients:**

**1 form of Holy Scripture Access**. (Traditional Bible, PC, Cell Phone or Tablet. Also, use which ever version of the Scriptures that you are comfortable with. I use KJV (King James Version), AMP (Amplified) and CEV (Contemporary English Version).

**1-4 Corresponding Scriptures**

**Proverbs 16:28 (CEV)** Gossip is no good! It causes hard feelings and comes between friends.

**Instructions:**

Decide on the date you will begin your behavior change. Count ahead 21-28 days and mark that date down. Now, commit to follow your plan for 21-28 days.

Write down your goal. List your reasons for changing or eliminating your habit. Find a substitute behavior. Talk to yourself. Reward yourself.

Remember to take one day at a time. Do as many "Appetizers" as you feel are necessary. Follow *your* "Meal Plan."

The appetizer section is to get you use to the "slow-cooking" process by working on a habit that seems minimal or easily workable. This section can really build your confidence and stamina for the more complicated courses which are to come.

Forgiveness is so important when undertaking this endeavor. I am speaking of the forgiveness of self. We are often times our worse critic.

I have developed a habit in which I choose to view my forgiveness toward mankind, myself included, as in relationship to God's forgiveness. Which is my desire as a father to forgive my own children. We cannot "out-forgive" God!

# How Did You Do Today?

(Use This Section to Record Daily Progress)

1 
_____

2 
_____

3 
_____

4 
_____

5 
_____

6 
_____

7 
_____

8 
_____

9 
_____

10 
_____

11 
_____

12 
_____

13 
_____

14 
_____

15 
_____

16 
_____

17 
_____

18 
_____

19 
_____

20 
_____

| 21 | |
| --- | --- |
| 22 | |
| 23 | |
| 24 | |
| 25 | |
| 26 | |
| 27 | |
| 28 | |

CHAPTER 4

## SOUPS AND SANDWICHES

### (A BIT FILLING BUT NOT OVERWHELMING)

*Ex:* Patience

**Prep time:** Dedicate at least forty-five minutes to find scripture(s) to support removing your old behavior and introducing the new. Also, if necessary, find a support person to cheer you on!

**Cook time:** 21-28 Days

**Ingredients:**

**1 form of Holy Scripture Access.** (Traditional Bible, PC, Cell Phone or Tablet. Also, use which ever version of the Scriptures that you are comfortable with. I use KJV (King James Version), AMP (Amplified) and CEV (Contemporary English Version).

**1-4 Corresponding Scriptures**

**2 Timothy 2:24** (CEV)

...and God's servants must not be troublemakers. They must be kind to everyone, and they must be good teachers and very patient.

**Instructions:**

Decide on the date you will begin your behavior change. Count ahead 21-28 days and mark that date down. Now, make a commitment to follow your plan for 21-28 days. Write down your goal. List your reasons for changing or eliminating your habit. Find a substitute behavior. Talk to yourself. Reward yourself. Remember to take one day at a time. Don't try to combine courses. Make affirmations, positive self-statements about your habit change. Follow *your* "Meal Plan."

Faith in God's Word will be your foundation. Understand the Bible as truth and the absolute Words of God. Have faith in your plan also. Take your time and be dedicated. This definitely takes devotion and discipline.

Remember, it is discipline that we are working on so if you have a fall back, keep it moving and don't give up! It is not only God's Word that is important but also its application. Continually apply new foundational ideas and scriptures to your life.

Try faith building exercises by randomly and purposely committing an act from you new behavior. Use these actions as sort of an inspection on your progress.

# How Did You Do Today?

(Use This Section to Record Daily Progress)

1

2

3

4

5

6

7

8

9

10

11

12

13

14

15

16

17

18

19

| 20 | |
|----|---|
| 21 | |
| 22 | |
| 23 | |
| 24 | |
| 25 | |
| 26 | |
| 27 | |
| 28 | |

CHAPTER 5

# DINNER CREATIONS

These will be your greatest tasks. This course may consist of addictions, traumatic experiences or something of the sort. The dinner course for some, may present itself as the one thing or set of things that you never wanted to be exposed.

Please be cautious with whom you invite to share this course with you. Do not be afraid to seek out professionals if it proves to become more than you are willing to conquer alone. Remember, you can conquer it!

**Romans 8:37** <sup>(AMP)</sup> Yet amid all these things we are more than conquerors *and* gain a surpassing victory through Him Who loved us.

Don't forget that we are slow cooking. We are not pressure cooking and when the going gets tough, the tough get going to get help.

*Ex:* Cigarette Smoking

**Prep time:** Dedicate at least one hour to find scripture(s) to support removing your old behavior and introducing the new. Also, if necessary, find a support person to cheer you on!

5 minutes per day dedicated prayer time.

**Research:** Use a search engine or reading materials to understand some of the negative impacts that your habit will have on your life and the lives of those connected to you.

**Cook time:** 21-28 Days; this is the actual act of laying down this particular habit for the specified time frame.

Ingredients:

**1 form of Holy Scripture Access**. (Traditional Bible, PC, Cell Phone or Tablet. Also, use which ever version of the Scriptures that you are comfortable with. I use KJV (King James Version), AMP (Amplified) and CEV (Contemporary English Version).

**1-4 Corresponding Scriptures**

Love for yourself

The desire for genuine change

The desire to follow God's Master Plan

Remind yourself that having to restart does not constitute a failure, only a true desire to see a change in your life.

Thomas Edison said, "Nearly every man who develops an idea works at it up to the point where it looks impossible, and then gets discouraged. That's not the place to become discouraged."

## On The Side

Sides are often over-looked and sometimes disregarded. For the sake of the Crock-pot Christian, sides add just a little fun to the meal.

Do something for yourself. Congratulate **YOU** for the efforts that you are putting forth! Invite those people that are helping in your courses to celebrate with you!

Whether, it is an evening at your favorite restaurant or a weekend at the beach. Just make it about your willingness to appreciate you.

You have decided to make plans to change your life around! You have decided that you want to be a true disciple of Christ!

Reward yourself for reaching milestones.  Example: This is my first complete week without being deceitful. I'm going to the movie theatre!

It's not about where you came from, but where you are going.

**Philippians 3:13**(CEV) My friends, I don't feel that I have already arrived. But I forget what is behind, and I struggle for what is ahead.

## How Did You Do Today?

(Use This Section to Record Daily Progress)

1 
_____
2 
_____
3 
_____
4 
_____
5 
_____
6 
_____
7 
_____
8 
_____
9 
_____
10 
_____
11 
_____
12 
_____
13 
_____
14 
_____
15 
_____
16 
_____
17 
_____
18 
_____
19

20 _____

21 _____

22 _____

23 _____

24 _____

25 _____

26 _____

27 _____

28 _____

CHAPTER 6

## SWEET ENDINGS

When you have finally laid aside all of your weights and sin; have a big ol' party!! Understanding that you have made a dramatic change in your life which warrants a gigantic celebration!

Moreover, you know that your new found discipline will show your character as "Christ-like" and as you continue it can only increase in value.

That's the self worth and value that others will find in you! After you finish each individual course, no matter how big or small just celebrate! You deserve it!

**2 Corinthians 5:17**
Therefore if any man be in Christ, he is a **new creature**: old things are passed away; behold, all things are become **new**.

**NOTE:** Every seven days give yourself an inspection. See where you are on your journey. Did I do, say or act in a way that would spoil my course? If not, great! If so, then encourage yourself to finish in grand fashion!

Alvin T. Harmon Jr.

THE PASTOR'S PRAYER FOR THE READERS

Father, I bring to you a people who desire to know the truth of you. Who have a willingness to understand what it takes to be pleasing in your sight and to walk in genuine Christianity.

I ask You to open wisdom and revelation to the readers of these pages. Strengthen them to overcome any hindrance(s) in their plight to form the discipline necessary to become Christ-like.

Bring peace to the frustrated vessels and hope to the discouraged heart. Send Divine healing. Reconstruct what has broken in the minds, hearts and spirit of your disciples.

In Jesus' name I ask. Amen.

*RECEPIE CARDS*

CUT, KEEP AND SHARE!!!

Alvin T. Harmon Jr.

Faith

Faith

Faith is being <u>sure</u> of what we hope for & <u>certain</u> of what we do not see. Heb 11:1

# Faith

IS TAKING THE FIRST STEP EVEN WHEN YOU DON'T SEE THE WHOLE STAIRCASE.

-Martin Luther King, Jr.

Patience

Patience

just because something isn't

happening for you right now

doesn't mean that it will never happen.

**Have patience with all things,**

**But, first of all with yourself.**

**-Saint Francis de Sales**

# Healing

# Healing

To everything there
Is a season.
A time for every
purpose under
heaven.

Ecclesiastes 3:1

If life gets
Too hard to stand...
KNEEL.

-Gordon B. Hinckley

Perseverance

Perseverance

"There is no such thing as
Instant spiritual transformation.
It is an ongoing process
Of ever-increasing glory.
Our character is transformed
Little by little, a bit at a time."
-Dave Earley,
*Living In His Presence*

# Perseverance
**Is the hard work you do
after you get tired of the
hard work you already did.
-Newt Gingrich**

## ABOUT THE AUTHOR

Alvin T. Harmon Jr. was born and raised on Maryland's Eastern Shore and began preaching and teaching at the age of twenty-five. His true-life experiences before and after salvation led him to learn by and foster his personal motto of; "Life just is; but be in a place to allow God to intervene."

This means that God is not personally responsible for everything which has happened or will happen in our lives.

Some things are due to a direct result of the decisions that we make. So we should plan to make good decisions.

He and his wife Tineka are the founders of Soul House Ministries Inc., of Maryland. Where they believe in serving the total man. His mind, body and spirit. The Soul's house!

They have dedicated their lives in ministry to perfecting the saints of God, through teaching life-application of the Holy Bible all over the United States.

For more information or prayer requests: send inquiries to soulhouseministries@live.com

***AVAILABLE SOON:***

The Crockpot Christian: *A Simple Guide To Christian Discipleship*

The Crockpot Christian: *Getting A "Flesh" Perspective*

Losing Control: *The End of Terror*

## The Crockpot Christian: *A Simple Guide To Christian Discipleship*

A workbook designed to help guide and motivate the "New Christian" through methodical discipleship. A look at a "slow-cooking" process to adopting new and removing old habits.

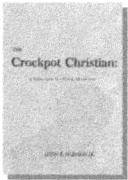

## The Crockpot Christian: *Getting A "Flesh" Perspective*

The flesh is believed to have "a mind of its own." Take a journey through the pages of this book to understand how to weaken and bring "flesh" into subjection.

## Losing Control: *The End of Terror*

Learn of a man's abusive character. See how he was able to "Lose his controlling nature" and end a cycle of domestic violence forever!

www.ingramcontent.com/pod-product-compliance
Lightning Source LLC
Chambersburg PA
CBHW060050050426
42448CB00011B/2392